Ελληνικά για μένα

.

Ελληνικά για μένα
Greek to Me

Joe Safdie

chax 2024

ISBN 978-1-946104-52-6
Library of Congress Control Number: 2024931794

First Edition 2024

Chax Press
6181 E Fourth St
Tucson AZ 85711
https://chax.org

Chax Press books are supported in part by individual donors and by sales of books. Please visit *https://chax.org/membership-support/* if you would like to contribute to our mission to make an impact on the literature and culture of our time.

We thank our current assistants, Erica Cruz and Ben Leitner, for their work on Chax projects. Our Art Director, Cynthia Miller, contributes to all books Chax publishes.

an oral consciousness operating with ambivalence
and not subject to the laws of contradiction

— *The Muse Learns to Write*, Eric A. Havelock

Contents

Introduction & Acknowledgments

This book is a selection of the poems I've written and published about Greek mythology since my first chapbook, while I was still an undergraduate at UC Santa Cruz in 1974. They're preceded by short introductions that identify their date and, sometimes, their context.

Many of these early poems first appeared in presses that no longer exist; indeed, one motivation for compiling them here was a sort of reclamation project. But some of the later ones were published by Geoffrey Gatza of BlazeVox Press (*Scholarship,* 2014), and Tod Thilleman of Spuyten Duyvil (*The Oregon Trail,* 2019) and are still very much in print; please check out these heroic small presses if you'd like to explore other work by me and many other writers worth your attention. A few other people, mainly teachers, are thanked in what follows; my wife Sara, my partner and companion through most of these explorations, I'll never be able to thank enough.

There are many speculations about why Greek myth retains its ability to seduce and inform, and I add to them here with a transcript of a recent talk I gave about the muses for the Centre for Myth, Cosmology and the Sacred in London. In my research for that talk, I came across one passage that I thought worth preserving, about my favorite Greek tragedy, *The Bacchae:*

Dionysus can take any shape he wants but is not fully visible to the human eye. He is a being who can successively and simultaneously appear as divine, animal and human. Pentheus defines the world through mutually exclusive antitheses and hierarchical relations. Man and woman, for example, are rigidly separate categories; each sex has its own sphere; one is subordinate to the other. Dionysus can simultaneously invert and subvert cultural categories: language, the roles of the sexes, classes and political hierarchy.

To understand Dionysus is to understand that the order imposed on the world by human culture is arbitrary, and the permanent potential for a reversal or collapse of this order exists.

— from *The Masque of Dionysus* by Helen P. Foley, 1980

The 1970s

This first poem is from my first chapbook, Wake Up the Panthers, *which came out when I was still an undergraduate at UC Santa Cruz in 1974; I was in my second quarter of accelerated Greek and knew enough to base the title on the Greek etymology for panther, namely "all beast," although I also had in mind Pan's ability to blend human and animal. The book was helped along by George Hitchcock and Kayak Press, but was more microscopic than small press: veterans of that world know such efforts often disappear completely. So it's amazing to me that the book was, not too long ago, on sale for $125 at Abe Books (I'd have let them have it for $50). Reading through it, I noted with some wonder that my style and concerns haven't really changed in close to half a century: for one thing, I still wear my teachers on my sleeve, in this case Ezra Pound, who was introduced to me that year by Norman O. Brown: I'll remember him in a few more pages. The epigraph to the poem is from Ken Kesey: "You're either on the bus, / or off the bus."*

The two small Greek translations that follow, from 1975, were the extent of my work in that field.

Odyssey on Route 101

And then went up to the bus,
set keel to breakers, forth on the godly
highway; my seatmate is reading Malcolm X,
a little late, but a real revolutionary
"is in the minds of the people," said Adams.
Watsonville, Salinas, Spreckles: Unreal.

For $15.20 the seamy side of America –
beer cans, billboards, dead animals,
smoky factories, truckers' cafes;
Husserl was never in Castroville, he
never smelled the artichokes – the mind
cannot function apart from sense, Edmund,

Le Paradis n'est pas artificial.
The lady next to me has horn-rimmed glasses
like old Cadillac tail-fins; jagged;
she speaks rapid Spanish to her daughter,
who is bored, world-weary in her plum-ripe
adolescence; she offers no response,

and the mother sighs, resigned: "Algun dia,
Algun dia" . . . Look! It's Aphrodite, there,
behind the gas station! She's come back
to us, Sappho, after 25 centuries! But
the bus ploughs on, grinding up the roadway,
the goddess left stranded, shivering in the cold.

Paso Robles – awkward youngsters embrace
by the burning lights of the Foster's Freeze,
oblivious to Time, and its chariot;
a fat lady (J.D.'s?) wearing a gray
checkerboard suit reads a mystery, not
knowing that the guilty one is the author . . .

Greenfield – a pimply naval officer,
prodded, stumbles off the bus, but no one
approaches to meet him; outside, the raindrops
explode on the windows, tiny bombs –
our crops remain barren, there is no
renewal; Zeus is just playing with himself.

Twisted oaks loom out into the blackness,
enticing – long, rough legs of a feminist.
Two blue-slippered feet brush my knee guiltily –
I mouth automatic assurances, look up,
and the tooth grin of an old woman
surprises us both; our eyes register

a common humanity, if our instincts
do not . . . Santa Maria, we've stopped here,
the driver's bladder is restless; silver
holiday lights are strung up over Main Street,
electronic magis to honor Christ;
"Little we see in nature that is ours" –

they've forgotten, again, about Adonis.
Pismo Beach – a palmist's advertisement
grasps empty air, yet her customers
won't be disappointed; for all is fated
in the lines . . . or in the stars . . .
the girls on the bus with the Sufi book know –

their cherubic faces, scrubbed clean
by meditation, show no trace of disorder,
but they show the same face to everyone.
Somebody tell Uncle William, there's
a vacancy in the Sully Gardens Hotel –
the rent for the night, though, is much too steep.

"But all this *really happened!*" taunts Martha;
the all-night drive in flashes images,
on the screen; kinesis, not mimesis.
And as the wide, flat road veers sharply
towards the west, a long-haired young man
writes words in the dark, molding his version

of the old American dream. It's his move;
all depends upon his choice, king or pawn;
but he's forgotten the rules of the game.

The Heart of the Matter

(from the Greek Anthology, anonymous, 4th century BC)

I fell in love, I kissed,
I got in, it was great,
now she loves me.

But who am I? And she?
And how . . .?
Only the god knows.

Advice to Males

(from the Greek of Agathias Scholasticus, 6th century AD)

If you have to love,
don't let go of the reins altogether,
and start blubbering
with your heart full of oily prayers.

Keep it inside.
Or at least raise your eyebrows,
and look at her
without giving it away.

Women only shake their heads
if you come on too strong;
and they'll laugh out loud
if they think you're crying.

The best lovers
know how to do both . . .
mixing their self-pity
with a little bit of pride.

The 1980s

Another early chapbook, Saturn Return, *came out from Smithereens Press soon after I moved to Bolinas, CA in 1983, and these next poems are from it. Again, I own what's certainly one of the last copies left of this book, with a cover illustration by the great Arthur Okamura (below). The book sought to confuse the myth of Saturn and the astrological Saturn with memories of my father. There was an epigraph to the chapbook from Rilke: "not one, one coming / but the countless ones teeming; not a single child, / but the fathers who rest in our depths / like the ruins of mountains."*

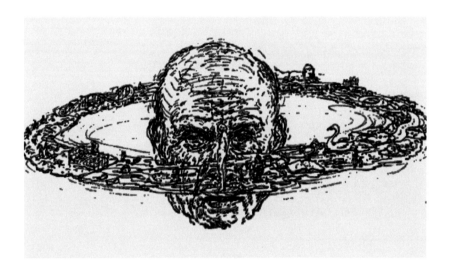

City o city
what was the name of that city
dark and obscure
    even in dream

So big as to be invisible
so monstrous
it eats its children
    every morning

Waking up in the city
Saturn just outside the window
    waiting to reclaim his throne

From the timeless
from the boundless
from the world of dream
    to the return of the god of time

        Saturn's transit of his own place
        is the most important point
        at which free will operates . . .
        you will not stand so free again

If you're not on the edge
you're in the middle
    lazy and respectable

Until he returns
your father who asks nothing
who stands quietly
    at the foot of your bed

§

My father had the biggest store on the block.
Only it wasn't a block and it wasn't his store,
and he drove fifty miles a day
for the privilege of working there –

through downtown, past the Yellow Pages sign
and a man in a tuxedo chasing termites
and onto the Santa Ana Freeway, where I stared
out the window and smelled the other cars –

the sweat of machines, the odor of oil drills,
Downey, City of Industry, determined faces
locked onto the freeway, my father's curses,
would we pass that little red car or not?

Then Lakewood Center, City of Commerce,
Brooks Brothers fights Rexall for dominion,
underground parking lots, wide shopping malls,
but always that smell of steel and oil . . .

That was how it was, father, when I
worked for you behind the register,
taking the customers' money, folding their clothes,
every minute was occupied, there was no spare time . . .

and I call you Saturn, master of work,
come down from the sky where you stay hidden,
come down with your crow's head and curved sword,
with your hourglass, your terrible sand.

§

Living in a large city
leaves you with yourself:
there's too much to see
outside your eyes.

You drift
in a becalmed ocean,
a Magellan who never made it
through the straits.

You think this is OK:
new world explorers
only found more of the same.

Saturn is dead.
His son, disguised as a swan,
drifts around somewhere
outside the city limits.

§

Film Noir

She was an accomplice to the crime, fashioned the weapon
from the hardest stone and gave it to her son, smiling like
Greta Garbo in *Grand Hotel.* Who could resist? When his father
came down later that night, hot and eager for his usual relief,
the boy jumped from the corner and split the old man's genitals
from his body with one clean stroke.

For a while no one spoke. Gods don't feel pain the way we do,
and never scream. They just stood there, the old man looking
down, the woman feigning surprise, and the kid feeling what
we call guilt, which hadn't been invented yet. It was time
for the Golden Age to dawn, but no one felt much like
celebrating. Finally the old man said "OK, you're the champ
now, I retire." Saturn said "Mama." Mama said "Go away boy,
I've got work to do."

§

Why did we leave the prairie?
I think it was California
that killed you,
great empty Paradise
that sucked off our midwest sheen
and spit us out,
stupid and alone in Hollywood.
Rumbling down Route 66
in our family Chevy,
we were a sixties parody
of *The Grapes of Wrath* –
refugees from Indian Country
and Rockefeller oil.

I stayed in the back seat,
my eyes fixed on the desert,
tracing the outlines
of cactus and sage;
sometimes my sisters would
shake me out of my trance,
it was my turn to guess.
Car games: 20 Questions, Geography,
Ghost. As we got near the ocean,
the speech we heard
sounded shriller and emptier,
like the quick flash
of a scythe in the wind.

§

I'm not your child.
I'm more like Mercury,
running every which way
trying to get the message.

Or maybe even Mars,
my temper as sudden
as a lighted match
in a dry forest.

But not yours.
I'm bored by your heavy lead,
that burden you carried
so long it broke you.

Even at the breakfast table
I doubted, figured
the scratches under your chin
were caused by your mask,

its sharp edges.
You weren't my father,
but someone else, some
impostor. That was why

you never spoke –
afraid of making a slip.
And later, baseball,
tying me to legends

that made all businessmen
anxious for summer –
you never complained when I
didn't take over the store,

your shyness was a shield
you hid behind
when I needed a clear signal,
anger, almost anything

but that lead coin you kept tossing,
apologizing for your birth
with every shrug.
Now you've retreated so far

even alchemists give up,
throw away their beakers
and get ordinary jobs
like everyone else . . .

and I'm still floating,
caught between lead and gold,
no sickle to point the way.

§

The Voyager Expedition

Ring around a dead planet,
there's nothing up there
but rocks and stones,
the same ones Rimbaud
had a taste for,
and Olson, dead at 60,
inflamed liver.

Now a ship named Voyager
speeds past Saturn
at a ridiculous rate –
the rate of the mind,
the speed Olson said
we need to put aside
for the sake of our lives.

Saturn in my life
has been a dying god –
the kind you associate
with scholarship.
Not once has he
appeared in my room while writing.
He doesn't command
any pyrotechnical displays.

When you're under his dominion
you don't feel
anything.

§

Visions of Saturn

I close my eyes and I see it –
all it is is a ring of steel;
a lion jumping through a hoop;
a picture of an old man
in an old-fashioned frame.

I close my eyes and I see it –
it's Paradise, the world
surrounded by a halo;
a basketball through a hoop;
a cord around a bushel of wheat.

It's what holds me back,
the boundary beyond which
I'm forbidden to wander –
it's the noose around my neck.

§

Saturn's Influence

We're standing in a line on stage,
your hands on my shoulders,
pushing me down.
The audience is restless,
they want to be entertained.

It's your turn to speak.
"This is my son, Joseph"
you say, your immigrant voice
a foreign vibration
in a sea of American chatter.

The audience starts laughing.
I can't see you,
want to drown from the shame,
feel the same grip
on my shoulders, constant,
keeping me up.

§

Saturn's Illness

Some family.
Brothers with fifty heads,
sisters with a hundred arms –

it's no wonder you
thought you had to eat me.
But I forgive your appetite.

I know how fear
makes you stuff yourself
so when you throw up
you can throw up the pain.

But it never works.
Those skinny women on Rodeo Drive
scare me more
than your stomach ever did.

§

Let's try it again –
I cut off your balls
and throw them as far as I can;
they explode when they hit the water,
and a beautiful woman
rises out of a shell.

I think you know that woman.
I see you in her eyes,
watch her struggle sometimes
beneath your lids.
I'm there too – we're actors
in a play about love.

Somebody else is speaking.
We're just waiting.

§

In the old days it was easy –
the father appeared
from out of the mist,
groaned a little,
and instructed the son
how properly to avenge
his tragic death.
There were a lot of swell
sound effects, a little wailing,
but destiny was clear.

Now the actors wander
all over the set,
forget their lines,
forget why they even
took the part.
The rewards are reduced
to a government check in the mail,
which keeps us happy,
the untranslatable language.

Shadows aren't important –
we can't see anything inside.
Sometimes we strain our eyes –
    Look, can you see anything? –
but everyone's gotten tired
of pretending they do.

Once, it was smoggy
and I couldn't breathe.
I sat back under a tree
and put my face to the ground,
scared of my dizziness.
When all the images stopped,
I heard your voice.

§

The medieval manuscripts
show you hunted, terrified,
swinging your sickle
at an unknown enemy;
or wounded, thinking,
lying back on your throne.

The night you discovered
I'd been doing drugs
the TV got turned off.
You acted as if
I'd made the fatal cut,
your eyes grew wild.

Finally, after hours
of pacing the floors,
growling some foreign tongue,
you managed some English:

> *Don't you understand*
> *everyone out there*
> *is against us?*

Father, we stayed so long
in that one corner of the room –
now you're dying,
your wheezing breath
and frightened eyes
spread through the skies.

I stand over your bed,
holding tight to your flesh,
wanting to heal.

The 1990s

September Song *was one of a series of fascicles published by Oasis Press publisher Stephen Ellis in 2000. Its main theme was time, focused through the lens of the month of September and whatever I could find out about it in history and mythology. As it turns out, the ceremony of Eleusis in Greece was held in late September, and that became the theme of three of these 20-line poems.*

in which several older personages are recalled

"September" is spattered with rape,
Kore dragged down
   into the Underworld, the Stolen Child –

Demeter, proud harvest-goddess,
   sees her own offspring
disappear – but is it for her daughter

that she wanders and wails
to the blank Olympian heavens,

   or herself – some wildness she'd thought
domesticated now, put away with the corn
into neat, geometric garden rows?

And with what awful mix of emotions
does she greet the news
   (there on the rock, slumped over)

that this rupture is now
  sanctified, called "seasonal"
be the latest young god

  and his PR staff? On this month
that makes so much of harmony, nothing
   to explain this loss . . .

    §

It's the *melancholy* that's the problem,
Saturn again, black humor, sense
of impending doom – the days
lose their light and monarchs,
resting on the way to Mexico,

proclaim what's left of summer . . .
Different than spring's promise,
first sprouts pushing through the soil –
mid-February, say, cold blasts of wind,
but the brightness, undeniable . . .

reincarnation is *based* on spring,
but "September" is Lawrence's
Ship of Death, the captain's log
crumbling, passengers staring
at nothing over the rail . . .

and the crew, the rest of us,
the ones who can't afford the Eleusis
Grand Tour? What do the oracles say?
Why do things get so colorful
before they're about to die?

§

Before the world dissolves
        in a blaze of particle physics,
the event horizon twisted,
impossible contortionist,
around our fragile frames

we could try to remember
        the old stories, before
the Big Bang, when Kore and her mother
were still one woman ... isn't *that*
        what Eleusis was all about,

isn't the Underworld the first
        black hole, and all the elegant theories
just different ways to stop *counting,*

to focus, finally, on only one
        pulse-point? Two women, one goddess:
a western koan, as September

circles back on itself, being
        instead of becoming, chronology
accepts design, and Kore falls
        beneath the western rim ...

The 2000s

In the late 1990s I became entranced with the Orpheus myth, as many poets have before and since, and worked intermittently on a serial poem called "The Story of O" for some 12-15 years. It was finally published in my first full-length book Scholarship *(BlazeVox, 2014); the epigraph to the poem was from my old teacher Edward Dorn's* Gunslinger:

> Then can you sing
> a song of a woman
> accompanied by that
> your lute which this
> company took to be a guitar
> in their inattention.
> Yes I can, but
> an *Absolute* I have
> here in my hand.
> Ah yes, the Gunslinger exhaled
> It's been a long time.

Three Figures (An Old Relief)

Hermes on the left, wearing
his invisible hat (which clearly
isn't working) looks somber,
cooling his wingéd heels,
laying down some law to Eurydice,
who can't believe her ears:
she has to stay in this pit forever
just because Orpheus looked back?
The lug (she's touching his shoulder
now) isn't quick, by any means
(wandering forlorn at her mere
disappearance into another world,
what used to be known as women's
prerogative), but he is solid, even
diverting in a way, the music . . .
"So what's in it for *me*, Herm?"
her large eyes flash con-
spiratorily, but He's the God
of messages, lady, the highest
possibility of same, and He's saying
"No way, sister, there's Other Forces
at work here" (already more
than most messages convey).
"Sex, death and art" says the
latest Rilke bio, i.e., there are
alternate readings, but none
that make Orpheus look *smart* –
of course he turns around,
his impatience pushing her

back into virginity,
a little too much in love
with his own music . . .
sorry, singer, but you got
the wrong message: it wasn't your song
that made the furies stop raging,
Sisyphus lie back on his stone.
Even in hell's ghostly shades
they remembered how it felt:
the last faint touch a lover leaves
before leaving us behind . . .

§

"a little too much in love
with his own music"

he'd gotten used
to the eyes closing,
bodies swaying in trance,

thought no one could resist
those melodies, sweeping
through the bloodstream,

swifter than any drug . . .
so challenged the death gods,
offered himself as well, and

the bloodless ghosts, too,
were in tears.* Triumphant,
he started back up,

but couldn't stop thinking about
the audience he'd just left,
command performance,

and looked back to see if there were
any more hangers-on . . .
someone should have told him:

you can't see the dead
by looking for them.
Soon the critics got restless,

dissing him like a pop star
whose second album sells
less than the first. They wondered

if he'd lost it, that unique sound,
that voice . . . he took to the hills,
becoming *the first of Thrace*
to prefer young boys* . . .
they never looked back

---

*Ovid's Metamorphoses, 10.55, 119-121

§

Or, the oar of discovery,
we were the first that ever
burst into that silent sea

Eurydice, how she falls,
silently, unredeemed, you're
rid of me now at last

Fee, the price he paid
for all of us (Ficino said
he *was* Jesus)   or "fey"

archaic, Scottish,
fated to die, having the air
of one under a doom or spell

Ear, how we heard the word,
by ear he said, or sense merely
*the obedient daughter of music**

Red, ease, the blood spurting
from the Maenads' rocks
ewe   rid   a   see

oar   fee   us
ear   red   ease
or fey

---

* Zukofsky, *Non Ti Fidor*

Orpheus Speaks

I don't trust these animals,
yellow eyes gleaming in the dark.
They'd just as soon rip me apart.

I don't know why I turned around –
I couldn't even see her face
in the dark. The villagers say

it was love, but Aphrodite
is not my god. She knows
I serve a different master:

order, harmony. What would happen
if I stopped playing this tune?
In the dark they'd rip me apart.

The drunken sailors on the ship –
all they remembered were the birds.
Did they ever find that fleece?

I was watching the birds. Order,
harmony. The dead liked it too,
their shadows were dancing.

Drunken sailors. Animals.
Aphrodite is not my god.
I didn't even see her face.

§

music, there's always
>*I don't want you to lose*

this music everywhere,
>*yourself, listen for*

a man can't hear himself think
>*what's not sounding*

drums pounding, bodies swaying
>*beneath your mind, the*

music's what drove her away
>*river, flowing, quiet*

drumbeats, pounding,
>*the musicians of death*

sirens, the scream
>*make the coolest sound*

§

O's Music

how Orpheus relates to women is
he charms them
tells them they're the one
sings *the hills are alive . . .*

they should have believed him
they thought it was *him* playing
when all he was doing
was allowing them   finally

    to listen
it seemed like nothing
they had ever heard before
their nervous

      systems
          collapsed

he was playing their death
and they called it love

§

Eurydice

It was a dream that you
rescued me, it was a dream,
our love . . . you never understood me,
always singing, singing,
as if a few strums from your lyre
could dissolve all the pain.
They told you it was a snake bite,

but not that my feet were bare.
I'd wanted to escape ever since
the astrologers told us
there were no exact aspects
for the day of our wedding
and the moon would be void of course.
You should have known too,

when Hymen's torch sputtered
and he wouldn't even look us
in the eyes, but you shrugged it off
(you shrug everything off)
as if he were another groupie
who didn't understand the sound.
Who knows why you came after me?

Maybe you wanted someone else
to notice your noble tears,
someone else who'd swoon
and tremble. You were
more comfortable in the mountains
than with me – I understand
why those women were angry

I understand why they tore you apart,
when all you gave them were those
raised eyebrows, that moony smile –
better the mad god than your
harmonizings, smoothings
around the edges . . . it's no good
to remember this now, we're stuck here,

wandering these shades forever.
Sometimes I even get a chance
to look back at you. And here's
what I see: no child, just your big eyes
and mincing steps. Are you
washing your hands again, dear?
Will you boil more vegetables tonight

or are we still fasting?
I hear that in the daylight
all they talk about now
is forgiveness. I want you to know
I don't forgive you –
no song you'll ever sing
will make me forget that fall.

§

three words
   are reserved
       only for him
poet   lover   failure

"stop deceiving the uneducated crowd
with empty sweetness" (*Metamorphoses* 5.308-9)
   aesthetically superficial
       ethically dishonest

warbling country tunes
   to nobody
rocks and stones and trees
       cold pastoral

     §

why didn't the snake
that bit Eurydice
hear the music?
in the Celtic version,

Sir Orfeo, it was fairy dust
that lured her down –
just back from the dentist
first time in thirty years

on nitrous oxide –
"Rocketman . . . burning out
his fuse up here alone"
lost in the stratosphere,

disembodied . . . was it
just dreaminess he offered,
his head floating
down the Hebrus,

the kind of poetry that
never made anything happen?

§

Orpheus Speaks (2)

I see it now: light.
Can she? Is she still there?
I can't even talk to her,
let alone look back . . .

how did they hear
my music below?
Strange here, nothing solid,
but nothing I don't know . . .

the silence before a poem.
Imagine *living* like that –
invisible. Communication
between souls. That was her soul

back there, the real woman,
her body rotting above: a summons
from all-powerful Day.
Watch: the invisible appears.

A mockery. A betrayal.

The 2010s

After Scholarship *was published in 2014, I certainly thought I could stop paying attention to the Orpheus myth, at least for awhile, but a few years ago the following short poem arose very quickly; it was also published in* The Oregon Trail (Spuyten Duyvil, 2021) *and appeared online in March 2022 on the* Poetry Daily *website.*

Orpheus Again

I smoke marijuana to return
       to the level of the stones –
or if not their splendid
  geological history
at least the surrounding
  shrubs and grasses
      dancing in place –

and that was the only secret
  to his music –
the real Orphics
  weren't so quick to imagine
      a way out of the world –
as the story has it
  this is it

for Norman Finkelstein

The Oregon Trail *contained four sections, one of which was called* "Hermes the Thief," *the title of Norman O. Brown's first book. Nobby (as everyone called him) made his reputation with the brilliant, uncategorizable books* Life Against Death *and* Love's Body, *but started his career as a classicist with this Marxist-influenced analysis of the elusive god. I enrolled in his class on Ezra Pound's Cantos in the fall of 1973, and nothing has ever been quite the same since. Almost all of my long poems (and sections of poems) have epigraphs, and this one is no different, from the book* The Greeks and the Irrational *by E.R. Dodds:*

> The recognition, the insight, the memory, the brilliant idea, have this in common, that they come suddenly, as we say, "into a man's head." Often he is conscious of no observation or reasoning which has led up to them. But in that case, how can we call them "his"?

from "Hermes the Thief"

poetry and magic
not the Spicer Circle
but the realm of Hermes
elusive   mercurial
kicking up chalk on the foul line

a dream address
everyone is there
already broken into groups
not chosen by lots
the lecture hadn't yet begun

if everything we see
is someone else's spell
sleight of hand
card tricks
when the world is the cards

§

there was a third way of living life,
besides the Apollonian rational
and the Dionysian irrational . . .
Hermes' way, the way of "roguery"

God of jokes and journeys, thieves
and magicians, the tricky Guide of Souls

Hermes the only one that is going
to rob you or enrich you,
enlighten you or screw you.

the split-second timing
the spirit of finding and thieving

---from Hermes: Guide of Souls *by Karl Kerenyi*
(introduction by Charles Boer)

§

to the accusation of theft
        Hermes would ask
    what is ownership

        §

Hermes also commerce
        intersection of ideas
three forks in the road
    I was the cashier
        at my father's clothing store
seed is soul

        §

Oregon Coast, Late May

my older books often explored
demarcated stretches of time

but now my muse is Hermes
   god of space-time
       offering Hermetic wisdom
while stifling a laugh

we must be moving on
   backwards or forwards
       not the relevant consideration

what takes place
   has no particular time

§

both Hermes' magical power to release
and the attendant power to bind
are illustrated in the so-called cursing tablets
inscribed with curses against persons named on them
and then buried in the ground

the Greek word for these tablets means "bindings"
and a number of them involve Hermes
as the one who holds down
or as we say   the spellbinder
(Brown, Hermes The Thief)

§

trickery means being alive
to metaphor   not just theft
stealth   not necessarily stealing
deception is required
coyote

§

muse, sing Hermes
the childish
the petulant
   taking pleasure
         in misfortune
the primitive
the phallic
the conniver
the magician
Autolycus
   with a god's quickness
the secretive
the scamp
the musician
pre-Olympian
   Titanic roots
      Atlas was his grandfather

§

the erect phallus
a magic wand
to turn away harm

god of primitive trade
rituals at the boundary
let there be commerce between us

Hermes allows us
to receive messages
from gods and other strangers

translating foreign tongues
evading walls
buying and selling at the border

both this and that
neither this nor that
coyote   serpent

"deceitful" only
if wedded to a position
any position

the necessity of deception
in all human activity
therefore I lie with her and she with me

in constant revolt
against reigning dispensations
trickery means being alive

not stealing but revealing
all writing works in secret
and any secret action

is magic
a god of moments
he just moves

you can't get a fix on him
standing outside
the armed camps of the gods

§

                    muse sing Hermes
the inconstant one
            human on my faithless arm
the breaker of oaths
slipping free from bonds
sliding from commitment
    ashes floating
            the disappeared

squirrel clambering along telephone line
speedboat down the Willamette

astrology is the Trismegistus part
the psycho-pomp
the system maker

Hermes is the squirrel

        §

                            Hermes' last trick in *The Iliad*
                            was spiriting Priam
                            behind enemy lines
                            to reclaim his son's body
                            giving humans a great gift

                            the full weight of their misery

The fourth and final section of The Oregon Trail *was called "Yachats, OR," commemorating (among a few other things), the coastal Oregon town of Yachats (specifically a ten-day vacation my wife and I took there in October of 2019). The books I took with me were the Collected Poems of Byron, Robert Kelly's* The Loom, *and a John D. MacDonald Travis McGee mystery, all of which figured in the poem; this was the final piece.*

Blank Document

I'm trying out the font "Athelas" in this piece
even though I'm sure it's another modern knock-off
and not something steeped in printing history –
I'll have to look it up
it does sound mythological
and I wanted to touch on those matters

because Jupiter and Saturn
are closer together in the skies
than they've been in 500 years –
on the Winter Solstice
they'll form a double star –
religious people will think of Jesus

but pagans will remember
Birth of Venus on my screen saver
born from the foam of the severed penis
cut off by Kronos the avenging son
with the sharp teeth of Gaia's sickle
"the excised manhood of Father Ouranos

fell into the restless sea, into which
Kronos had cast it from the firm earth"
"and since the bloody deed of Kronos
the sky has no longer approached the earth
for nightly mating"   and people think *Trump*
is destructive   anyway this week

Kronos reunites with his son Jupiter
(switching now to Roman terminology)
both squaring Venus in my astrological chart
and tonight is probably the clearest sky
we'll have in Portland for two weeks
so I'll interrupt the poem at this point

and see if I can see them   as they are now
a degree apart in late Capricorn

[third line left blank in honor of experience
amid poetry's absurd quest to capture the real
and the hope that negative space is generative]

reading now from du Beauvoir's *Second Sex*
where she quotes Byron from *Don Juan* (!)
"Man's love is of man's life a thing apart;
'Tis woman's whole existence"
a passage whose sexism I at first rejected
but find that du Beauvoir agrees completely

with Byron about the slavish surrender
that love is for women   and which Kelly
in *The Loom* and Chernicoff's essay
is at pains to demystify   I don't know the story
of his separation from Helen
but she infuses the poem as her forebearer did

Homer's essentially masculine world
brought to a 19th century gloss by Byron
and that's also what "Yachats" is about
that and the survival of Greek mythology
into 21st century poetry and poetics
meanwhile, what do you think of Athelas?

Regular *Italic* **Bold** ***Bold Italic***
I was right it's an Adobe font
created in the historic year 2008
"inspired by British fine book printing"
"included as a system font in Apple's
macOS operating system" in other words

about as far from mythology as you can get
"named after a healing herb
in Tolkien's *Lord of the Rings*" well
some people don't even *have* a history
and now to return to Venus on her shell
Wynd's *Pagan Mysteries in the Renaissance*

at hand for elucidation along with *The Loom*
its awkward early seventies vernacular
at times disguising its spiritual quest
the narrator a seeker of good poetics
(like starting the poem with its typeface)
whatever lies at hand an e-mail from Kent

arrives about his latest Facebook post
he told me that one of my recent poems
had the most surprising ending since Rilke's
"You must change your life" (doesn't that
make you want to read it?)
I'll read his post but first listen

to Van Morrison's *Poetic Champions Compose*
which might be a theme of this poem
it turns out Botticelli's *Birth of Venus*
was a commission job   one Pierfrancesco
cousin of Lorenzo the Magnificent
and student of Ficino and Politian

too bad those appellations went out of style
I'd like to call my friends (on occasion)
"Magnificent"   or "Ludicrous"   or both
as in many of Kent's Facebook posts
the first cut "Spanish Steps" was instrumental
and totally divine   "Morrison follows his muse

wherever he likes. And every time, those
who have committed themselves to the journey
have been rewarded"   (*Rolling Stone,* 1987)
the lyrics to the second cut "The Mystery"
include "I saw the light of ancient Greece
Towards the One / I saw us standing

within reach of the sun"   except
in Portland   where the sight last night
of golden Saturn above and to the left
of brilliant Jupiter will have to be
the last I see with unaided sight
"There's a dream where the contents are visible /

where the poetic champions compose"
sings Van   almost as inscrutable
as Edgar Wynd writing about Venus
but Venus is always there
just about to step off the shell
and explode in your heart forever

even when you think it's not shattered
shards and fragments come from nowhere
fierce stabs at the heart for the love not given
What are the overlooked changes
that have emerged from technology?
"A negative change is a tendency

to trust technology too much . . .
The ultimate Hollywood example
of dystopian tech is *Wall-E* – technology
making everything so easy that we lose
our personal agency"   six years
from Carr's *The Glass Cage* and counting

campaigns begin for the vaccine
rural Americans tell science to fuck off
"COVID=HOAX"   the name of a Hearts player
on my phone app   polio redux
Robert Kennedy runs for president
the sun and Mercury trine my Venus

memories of the *Homeric Hymn to Hermes*
providing relief from the Zeus-Kronos Square
breaking news   the clouds might part tonight
to see Zeus inch ever closer   laying in wait
preparing the poison   ultimate momma's boy
his brothers and sisters swallowed

Goya's tremendous painting
"the great Kronos   the tortuous thinker"
that from this sexual violence love would arise
is a myth that needs further inspection
"That's a wrap on TechfestNW 2020 –
Portland's signature event that celebrates

the entrepreneur in all of us. This year
due to COVID, TFNW had to pivot
their originally planned in-person event
to a virtual platform"   Google & Facebook
under fire from the Feds
like Microsoft was   you remember Microsoft

feared economic monopolist
now all they have left is Word
which I'm *not* knocking
I've always found it more useful
than other programs I've tried
and it's more portable than Adobe

who made the font I'm using in 2008
inspired by British fine book printing
like the cantos of *Don Juan* when they appeared
serially   close to when Byron wrote them
spontaneity a model then as now
Keith Jarrett in the background

there were people who thought
that he wasn't important
not on the same level as Miles or Coltrane
I'll tell you in a minute once I listen
first I heard "If This is Goodbye"
from Mark Knopfler and Emmylou Harris

the occasion some stanzas back for
intense emotional regret at lost love
which turns out to be Knopfler's tribute
for the victims of 9/11!   see, there's a place
for criticism   and the best critics
like Northrop Frye   are hanging with Blake

in a portal of the sky
an ad for iPhone Pro Max
at the top of my Facebook ads
makes me momentarily forget
recent ads in the *New York Times*
where Facebook excoriated Apple

one hysterically ending "StandUpForSmall"
"Great Kronos devoured all his children as soon as
each of them had left its mother's sacred womb . . .
he did not wish any other god to succeed
to his possession of this dignity"
the Golden Age in his belly   he threw it up

after being fed peyote by Jupiter
which led to all the other Ages
pandemics   wars   endless violence
some say the conjunction will end all that
but Jupiter has moved on   past the castrator
what was that about the Christmas star?

to the memory of Kent Johnson

The 2020s

This next sequence is a series of short poems, a bit like the Saturn poems, called "Praise for the Muses"; they arose from a talk I gave about the Muses last autumn for the Centre for Myth, Cosmology & The Sacred in London in 2021, a transcript of which follows these poems.

Praise for the Muses

the thing about ancient poetry
is that it wasn't
just poetry

we're a long way away from those times
those times were too

§

the Muses are invisible
but allow us to sing
while they dance
covered in mist
at the boundary
of oral and written

§

among the more ancient powers
singing and dancing
older parts of the brain

a party at the beginning
of written language
memory shattered by thunder

nine nights he went to her
the lyre soothing the eagle
even the god of war was pacified

§

Mnemosyne   ne moss enay
was a Titan
appearing very early on the scene
as if the first things humans do
is remember what they did

§

when the Muses dance
stately   measured
it's possible to imagine
virtue   order
they're not Maenads
but resemble Sirens
don't you want to hear
their sweet singing

§

gold hairbands
gold sandals
handsome houses
clear eyed
sweet   light
harmonious
not themselves
called wise

§

memory   minded again
first song by Hermes
on the lyre he invented
was praise
for the mother of muses

§

69

Terpsichore at my wedding
but also at Smiley's –
"you're a good dancer!"
she said with surprise –
and bumping asses
with that red-headed secretary
at a work party
and at the community center
with the woman
who would become my wife
gliding across the floor
to Sexual Healing

§

Blake said that the muses
Plato worshipped
were daughters of memory
rather than imagination
but Plato didn't really worship them
and the muses
wanted nothing to do with him

§

Erato I know mainly
through absence
take care of my heart
she told me once
did I always mean
to tear the paper in half
faint pink of sunrise
false promise of dawn
the minor aches that
never quite go away
like I'll never hurt you
"my errors are many
my lies numberless"

§

they're beyond you
and right behind
inhabiting the moment
isn't good enough
Clio's secret name is loss

§

the joys of gods
the sufferings of humans

§

I met Urania when I saw
clouds streak across the sky
and woke up everyone at home,
screaming "The sky is moving!"

I was five. Then, on the late shift,
a fellow typesetter told me
I was about to experience
my first Saturn Return –

40 years of astrological study
followed, while Urania –
"of grave and serious mind" –
keeps looking

somewhere in the stars
for perfect patterns and rhythms,
holds back sometimes
in the midst of the dance

§

the muses sing for the rulers
it doesn't matter who they are
they mix lies with truth
"the fame of past and future"
effortless smoothness
 the song flows from their mouths
their hearts yearn for it
soothe your troubles   forget your sorrows
grant me gifts of lovely song
the laws and customs of immortals
graves and desire close at hand

§

Byron's epitaph in *Don Juan* –
"Hail Muse, etc." – was preceded
by Persius, first century AD:
"The maidens of Mount Helicon
and the blanching waters of Pirene
I give up to the gentlemen round whose busts
the clinging ivy twines; it is only
as a half-member of the community
that I bring my lay to the holy feast of the bards"

§

boss Calliope
mother of Orpheus
often holding a lyre
poetry is "Calliope's screeching"
wrote Dionysius Chalcus
scolded by Aristotle
for the bad metaphor

§

Sappho the tenth muse –
her curse to the unbelievers:
you have no share
in the roses from Pieria
but in the House of Death also
you shall walk unseen
with the insubstantial dead

§

Polymnia   also known
as a ministering angel
and messenger of the Most High

come in peace, angels of peace
shabbat is the shekinah
in any congregation

even the one where I was enveloped
by men with smelly cigar breath
saying "give it to the kid to hold"

the place where first they set me
on the path of clear song
(Works and Days)

where the visible and invisible meet
isn't a place –
it's an attitude

a recitation of sounds
as light as the air
that carries them

This last fairly recent poem owes its existence to a rereading of Karl Kerenyi's Eleusis *along with a book unaccountably neglected by me for many years,* Charles Stein's brilliant Persephone Unveiled.

Eleusis

> The different ways of writing her name on Attic vases
> may disclose a fluid situation somewhere
> between utterance and concealment. --Karl Kerenyi

two goddesses become one
at Eleusis in September
Demeter turned towards the light
her daughter towards death

> "in a single figure which was *at once*
> Mother and Daughter, she could . . .
> combine the feminine attributes of the earth
> with the inconstancy of the wandering moon."

the lesser mysteries in spring
only a preparation

§

Persephone rises
like baseball half the year
lately disfigured by wildfires
drought   war crimes   genocide
she might as well have stayed below
where labor disputes are invisible

Persephone has no personality
always the lost one
the gap in the pattern
nagging feeling of loss
she must have been here
because she sure feels gone

Persephone loved her mother
but never let her know
most of her life was underground
the only things that surfaced
were hard to decipher
summits of sunken mountains

Persephone not like her mother
or Gaia or any other
earth goddess
she rules the underworld
invisible
imaginary

Persephone never forgot
her ancestry was clouded
Pan and Dionysus involved
and her mother was a Titan
the first one who fucked Zeus
the muses were her sisters

she can't be seen
she only smiles
nobody speaks her language
the blooms are miraculous
only because of
what can't be uttered

one of the ancient ones
makes the voice falter
the only goddess
described as ineffable
the poets preferred to speak of her
without a name

This concluding essay is an attempt to get at the themes of the poems in another form; it's a transcript of a talk I gave on Zoom for the Centre for Myth, Cosmology & The Sacred in London in October of 2021 (minus a few power-point slides), and I want to thank here its founders, Mary Attwood and Louise Livingstone. It's probably harder to evoke a sense of the Muses in prose than it is in poetry, but perhaps having the two in one place will enable them to ricochet off each other.

Musing about The Muses

"Could you completely forget yourself
even for an instant, you would be given everything"
---an epigraph from the 13th century German mystic Meister Eckhart

Thank you, Mary [Attwood], and thanks to the Centre itself for being one of my muses since I discovered it last year . . . and in very specific ways, in that the last several presentations I've seen on the Centre website, including yours just last week on the art of memory, all seem to have said what I want to say today much more cogently. So in that sense, thanks especially to William Rowlandson on the wild, Mark Vernon on Dante and Patrick Curry on Enchantment in the past months: all of these should be available on the Centre website, or soon will be. And, of course, thanks to all of you here on Zoom; there should be plenty of time at the end for questions and comments, but don't be shy about using the chat box as we go further.

So if I had monitored the publicity for this talk tonight a little more closely, I might have de-emphasized the concept of inspiration and instead called it something else, like "Embedded Cognition, Metaphor and the Muses," because what I'm *not* going to do is offer a self-help session in learning how to be more creative in your daily life or pretend I know anything about "invoking your personal muse." I actually downloaded an article last month with exactly that title, because I thought it might have something I could use tonight, but it wasn't to be. In fact, the Muses aren't very good role models for developing self-esteem: when they first greet Hesiod in his *Theogony,* they call him "a poor fool" and "nothing but a belly," and proceed to tell him that they lie all the time . . . but can tell the truth when they want to. If that sounds a little capricious, remember that many of the gods and mortals of Greek mythology act in exactly the same way.

> from Hesiod's Theogony

> You shepherds of the wilderness, poor fools,
>   nothing but bellies,
> we know how to say many false things
>   that seem like true sayings,
> but we know also how to speak the truth
>   when we wish to.
>   (ll. 26-28, tr. Richmond Lattimore)

Still, some very great poets, as we'll see, seemed to need what the Muses were selling. So what was that? For one thing, it was as much information as inspiration, and it had a lot to do with memory, and metaphor, and both together. Their genealogy was important: genuine goddesses, their father was Zeus, but their mother was Memory – Mnemosyne in Greek – so metaphorically (and it's hard to speak about the Muses without metaphor), the Muses are

80

memories charged through with thunderbolts. And those kinds of memories don't only concern the past; when we're reminded of someone, or something, we're exactly that: re-minded, *minded* again in the present, with the opportunity to make things new. It's in that sense that the Muses "tell of what is, and what is to be / and what was before": they're bridging the past and present, metaphors for metaphorical thinking itself. When poets invoke them – re-call them – they're asking for the chance to amplify those past stories in the voices of the present. "Make my poem bigger," they ask; "let it encompass more of the world than I'm able to alone."

Eric Havelock, whose book *The Muse Learns to Write* is one of the main resources for this talk, wrote in it "Not creativity, whatever that may mean, but recall and recollection pose the key to our civilized existence." And my old teacher Ed Dorn, in an early statement for the Paterson Society, wrote "Culture is based on what men remember, not what they do . . . Even a civilized man who can read and write will occasionally exhibit this memory, at which times it is said of a man he acted with loveliness." The classics scholar E.R. Dodds, in a great book called *The Greeks and the Irrational,* had this to say about the action of the Muses:

> Just as the truth about the future would be attained only if man were in touch with a knowledge wider than his own, so the truth about the past could be preserved only on a like condition. Its human repositories, the poets, had (like the seers) their technical resources, their professional training; but *vision of the past, like insight into the future, remained a mysterious faculty, only partially under its owner's control, and dependent in the last resort on divine grace* (81). (My italics)

Finally in this introduction, the American poet Jack Spicer is the poet most beholden to the practice of dictation from the outside that I know of – although he called those voices "Martians" and not Muses – and I'll come back to an important lecture he gave in Vancouver in 1965 a little later on, but here's just one snippet that rhymes with the ideas I've mentioned so far:

> In the long run, the past and the present and the future are pretty much the same kind of furniture in the room. Just because a thing happens tomorrow that is in the poem today doesn't really mean that there's anything more mysterious than something that happened yesterday being in the poem today. I mean, the future, the past and the present are in some ways entangled. I don't know how, but they are . . .

So with that entanglement in mind, here are the topics I want to touch on today before we open things up for your comments and questions. I'm halfway through my introduction:

I   Introduction to the Muses

II   Invoking the Muse: The Roll Call of Poets

III   Embedded Cognition and Hesiod

IV   Conclusion: The Muses and the Wild

That is, after a quick dive into the poetic history of the muses, we'll come back to Hesiod's *Theogony* – the most extended description of the Muses and their work that we have – and also, less traditionally, his *Works and Days.* That latter poem features what we might call "embedded cognition," a neuro-scientific term that basically means letting the world and immediate environment in as part of one's thought, which, as Iain McGilchrist has shown us, activates the right hemisphere of the brain:

> gods were seen at the implicit level as aligned in some sense with the self, however distinct they may have been at the explicit level . . . sudden thoughts and emotions are seen both as the intervention of personal deities and at the same time as an aspect of independent human psychology. (*The Master and His Emissary*, 265)

McGilchrist adds "The crux is that the two planes exist in harmony, and the god's intervention need not imply that the mortal man is less fully responsible for his actions. Similarly poetic skills come from oneself *and* from the gods; and, in general, thought comes from oneself *and* from divine prompting." Or as my friend the poet Charles Stein wrote on *Facebook* in August, "Hesiod's evocation of the muses is neither in the active voice indicating masterful agency nor complete passive voice receptivity, but middle. Hesiod says the muses 'blew a singer's voice into (his) own.'"

Speaking of singing, it's a shame that I don't have a soundtrack for you, because for the Greeks, the Muses *were* music, all aspects of it, including singing, dancing, festivals, celebrations . . . and poetry; in fact, all of the ancient Greek poetry we read and study today was set to music, and the Greek word *Musa,* with a capital "M," is the same as the small "m" *musa,* music. Music, after all, came before words: it *was* "the oral tradition," and the Muses had been alive for centuries on the lips of oral bards and singers and storytellers before appearing in the first written poems of Homer and Hesiod. But I do have a snippet of what that music sounded like, and by great good luck, it's a song-poem that starts off with an invocation to the Muses (*https://www.youtube.com/watch?v=SgpWXDSSHEo*). You can see the lyrics translated into English at the bottom.

There are quite a few stories in Greek mythology about the Muses having contests with other singers, all of which they won, and they weren't exactly grateful winners: I'll mention a famous one in a few minutes. But it's important to remember the time of the poems; in a sense, the Muses were the guests of honor at a party at the beginning of written language, the Homeric and Hesiodic poems, and that wasn't really very far away, not before 700 B.C.E. The oral memory, aided as it was by rhythm, harmonies, and gestures, was very different than the literate souls we've all become. As Walter J Ong wrote, in *Orality and Literacy*:

> Persons whose world view has been formed by high literacy need to remind themselves that in functionally oral cultures, the past is not felt as an itemized terrain, peppered with verifiable and disputed "facts" or bits of information. It is the domain of the ancestors, a resonant source for renewing awareness of present existence, which itself is not an itemized terrain either. Orality knows no lists or charts or figures.

And, of course, neither did the Muses. But again, I want to disabuse us of the notion that the Muses are some kind of mystical, other-worldly personages: metaphor, after all, is actually very concrete, very here-and-now. Here's Havelock again, in his earlier *Preface to Plato*:

> The evocative effects described by Hesiod and prefigured as the gift conferred by the Muse were not a spiritual transfiguration, but a set of psychosomatic mechanisms exploited for a very definite purpose. Their effective employment required a degree of virtuosity in the manipulation of verbal, musical and bodily rhythms which was extreme.

And rhythm, he writes elsewhere, is "the foundation of all biological pleasures – all the natural ones, sex included – and possibly of the so-called intellectual pleasures as well." Be that as it may, it's the opposite of the more well-known theory of poetic inspiration brought to us mainly by Plato: as he saw it, the functional purpose of poetry as tribal education was being transferred to prose, so the people who thought in prose – that is, philosophers – needed to relegate the poetic experience to something non-conceptual, non-rational and non-reflective. It was a kind of ecstatic possession, wrote Plato, and that's why he kicked poets out of his ideal republic … and when they left, they took the Muses with them.

Invoking the Muse

The Muses Dancing on Mt. Helicon (1807. Berthel Thorvaldsen. Danish. 1770-1844. Marble.)

Most of us know the Muses as forces to be invoked, or called (or re-called), at the beginnings of epic poems. An invocation is often a prologue to the events to come, a prayer of sorts, usually made to one of the nine muses of Greco-Roman mythology; I'll show you their names in a minute. The poet asks for the inspiration, skill, knowledge, or the right emotion to continue with the poem. So, in *The Odyssey,* Homer asks for inspiration and a blessing for the retelling of the epic:

> Speak, Memory – of the cunning hero the wanderer,
> blown off course time and again
> after he plundered Troy's sacred heights.

So in that translation at least, the muse *was* memory. But it's important to remember that other Homeric invocations of the Muses came before detailing a complex catalog of ships, or, in *The Iliad,* in the midst of ferocious battles, with mangled limbs strewn around the battlefield, and suddenly the poet says "Speak, Muse, of the first Achaean to seek revenge," an example of asking for one's memory to be refreshed, so the poet can go on with his or her tale. I don't have time today to go into the intricacies of what's been called "the Homeric question," but the work of Millman Parry and people who came after him have pretty much established that Homer's poems were full of stock formulas and phrases, dependent on the meter of the particular line they occur in, rather than inventions: calls to the Muses were no different.

We'll come back to ancient Greece and Hesiod, but the Muses also figure in a famous contest with some rival singers that they turn into magpies in Ovid's *Metamorphoses*. And that story, in turn, is recalled in Dante's *Divine Comedy,* at the beginning of the *Purgatorio*:

> But here let my dead poem rise again,
> O sacred Muses! for it's you I serve,
> and here too let Calliope rise a little
>   so that she may accompany my song
> with that same sound that hit the wretched magpies
> so hard they lost all hope of future pardon. (I, 7-12)

That's a new translation that I can recommend by D.M. Black, and I wanted to quote it here for two reasons: 1) it remembers the dual function of the Muses, not only to serve as inspiration for the rest of the poem, but as a reminder that they're not particularly nice, and have no compunctions about being violent with anyone who might claim poetic skills without their guidance; and 2) at the beginning of this second book, Dante and Virgil are walking against the stream of Lethe, or forgetfulness, the river that works against what the Muses do. One final connection with Dante's poem that might be relevant is the difference between the *Inferno* and the *Purgatorio,* in that the characters in the first work are fixed in their sins forever – literal vision, or what Blake called "single vision and Newton's sleep" – while the *Purgatorio* reviews those exact same sins as opportunities to repent, or move on, as in allegory. So again, the Muses are acting as metaphors for metaphor itself.

Shakespeare's most famous mention of the Muses might be in *Henry V,* "O for a Muse of Fire that would ascend the highest heaven of invention" but he also performed an on-again/off-again dance with them in Sonnet 38:

> How can my muse want subject to invent
> While thou dost breathe that pour'st into my verse
> Thine own sweet argument, too excellent
> For every vulgar paper to rehearse? ...
> Be thou the tenth muse, ten times more in worth
> Than those old nine which rhymers invocate;
> And he that calls on thee, let him bring forth
> Eternal numbers to outlive long date.
> If my slight muse do please these curious days,
> The pain be mine, but thine shall be the praise.

Here Shakespeare prefers his human lovers, male here and female in the later "Dark Lady" sonnets, to the somewhat dubious realities of the classic muses. Likewise, in *Othello,* the villainous Iago complains of his own lack of "invention" and says, "My muse labors, and thus she is delivered," thus drawing a parallel between literary creation and childbirth.

Things changed again with John Milton's *Paradise Lost*:

> OF Mans First Disobedience, and the Fruit
> Of that Forbidden Tree, whose mortal taste
> Brought Death into the World, and all our woe,
> With loss of *Eden*, till one greater Man
> Restore us, and regain the blissful Seat,
> Sing Heav'nly Muse ...

Milton is still invoking the muse, or muses, to inspire him to write his epic poem, but *Paradise Lost* is a re-telling of the first book of Genesis in the Old Testament, so the muse now switches identities and becomes the Holy Spirit who inspired the Christian Bible, not one of the nine classical muses in Hesiod. Milton wanted his muse to fly above those muses because he was writing about the creation of the Bible and the universe; in that, *Paradise Lost* is a direct descendant of Dante's *Commedia* (although Hesiod was writing about the creation of the universe as well). But like those previous poets, Milton had a prodigious memory: one of the most amazing things to remember about him is that he didn't write *Paradise Lost,* he dictated it from memory, like the blind Homer taking dictation from oral singers.

Moving through the pantheon of great poets, here's William Blake, in a 1799 letter:

> [I] cannot previously describe in words what I mean to design, for fear I should evaporate the spirit of my invention . . . And tho' I call them mine, I know that they are not mine, being of the same opinion with Milton when he says that the Muse visits his slumbers and awakes and governs his song when morn purples the East, and being also in the predicament of that prophet who says: "I cannot go beyond the command of the Lord, to speak good or bad."

Finally, even though the Romantic poets as a whole aren't the best place to look for evidence of the Muses because of their idealization of the poet, we shouldn't forget Keats' notion of negative capability – "when one is capable of being in uncertainties, Mysteries, and doubts, without any irritable reaching for fact and reason" – nor this lovely quote by Shelley in his *Defense of Poetry*: "The mind in creation is as a fading coal, which some invisible influence, like an inconstant wind, awakens to transitory brightness."

And the Muses haven't disappeared with contemporary poets either: here are two.

Norman Finkelstein: The muse – and the Outside, and hearing voices –is a metaphor for the important listening that a poet has to do. If it's not from the outside, it's from the inside, from the unconscious – but that's unreachable: stuff wells up, and then you work it.

Ed Dorn: There are certain Obligations of the Divine, whether those can be met or not. Part of the function is to be alert to Spirit, and not so much write poetry as to compose the poetry that's constantly written on air. What I've read and what I hear merge to make the field in which I compose.

All of this is a way, writes another poet, Don Byrd, to experience "the richness of the world apprehended without the habits of recognition." Finally, I mentioned Jack Spicer a few minutes ago as the poet most beholden to outside dictation. He started a lecture in Vancouver, Canada on June 13, 1965 – the 100th anniversary of William Butler Yeats' birth – by talking about Yeats' wife channeling what Spicer calls "spooks." But these voices weren't there to offer any self-help advice; rather, they came, they said, in a response to Yeats' question, to give him metaphors for his poetry. Spicer has a number of juicy quotes relevant to this talk but, for reasons of time, I can only offer a few of them: "But occasionally, after an hour or so of me trying to write the poem . . . a poem nudges me on the back and starts coming through"; or this – "you have the alphabet blocks in your room: your memories, your language, all of these other things which are yours which they rearrange to try to say something they want to say. They are using my memories"; or this – "You have to keep a kind of lookout for them. You can't catch them like canaries by putting salt on their tails, but you sort of give them an even chance. I mean, show them there's a good dinner of blood like in *The Odyssey* where they dug the trench and slit the throats of the sacrificed animals." Ultimately, he says, what's important is "just cleaning things up so that the invaders, the things which are parasitical on you and create poems, can come in." Anything which takes us out of the trap of the personal, he says, is a good thing.

You might think that as the centuries roll on, we would see shifts from dependence on deified inspiration to the development of personal insight, and we do in fact see glimpses of that, culminating, somewhat hilariously, with Byron's introduction to a canto of *Don Juan:* "Hail muse, etc." But Byron was preceded by a gentleman named Persius in the first century C.E.:

> The maidens of Mount Helicon
> and the blanching waters of Pirene
> I give up to the gentlemen round whose busts
> the clinging ivy twines; it is only
> as a half-member of the community
> that I bring my lay to the holy feast of the bards.

So from the very beginning, there were people who thought they heard the voices of the Muses, and others, like Aristophanes, who were sure those people were deluded. But I want to end this little survey by quoting some lines from someone who did believe in the muses, Sappho. These recovered lines seem like a curse:

> you have no share
> in the roses from Pieria
> but in the House of Death also
> you shall walk unseen
> with the unsubstantial dead

The Specialties of the Muses

The Muses Dancing around Apollo (Baldassare Peruzzi, unknown date. WikipediaCommons.)

Calliope – "she of the beautiful voice" – was widely revered as the goddess who inspired epic poems and songs. The mother of Orpheus, she was often considered the most powerful of the Muses: Milton criticized her for not being able to save Orpheus from the maenads. But Calliope's eight sisters each had spheres of influence and were important in their own ways. The other Muses, as named by Hesiod, were:

Kleio – "the giver of fame," "Celebrator"; the Muse of history, she inherited the memory of past events from her mother, Mnemosyne.

Euterpe – "the giver of joy," "Delighter"; like Calliope, associated with music and poetry. Her specialty, though, was lyric poetry that told personal stories instead of epic tales of the past; mistress of the flute.

Erato – "the awakener of desire," "Enrapturer"; her name meant "desired" or "lovely" and was related to that of Eros; the goddess of love poetry and the dance.

Melpomene – "the singer," "Song Player"; one of the two Muses of theatre, she inspired the playwrights and actors of elegies and tragedy; also associated with lyre playing.

Thaleia – "the festive," "Luxuriator"; the counterpart of Melpomene, she inspired theatrical comedies.

Urania – "the heavenly," "Heaven Dweller"; she gave inspiration to astronomers. In the later years of the Roman Empire she was said to inspire Christian poetry.

Polymnia – "she of many hymns"; hymns, or poems of praise, were her specialty. She was also a mathematical muse who inspired work in geometry; a storyteller.

Terpsichore – "she who enjoys dancing," "Dance-Delighter"; the Muse of dance. She also gave inspiration to the chorus in Greek theatre; associated with the lyre.

While I was writing this talk, my wife asked me a question I couldn't answer: why were the Muses all women? If any of you have ideas, please say so at the end; I think it's probably too easy to say that ancient Greece was a culture where women were subservient. Anyway, according to Karl Kerenyi, "Whenever they went in procession to Olympus, they were wrapped in clouds. One could only hear their wondrously beautiful voices in the night." And with all this focus on being hidden, it might not be surprising to hear another famous story regarding the Muses: they gave the Sphinx its riddle.

Embedded Cognition and Hesiod

As I mentioned, the *Theogony* wasn't the only poem of Hesiod's we read today; there's also *Works and Days,* at first glance far away from "creative inspiration," in that it's the record of a farmer and the different things good farmers have to do throughout the year, one of which was to keep track of the weather and observe the skies. It demonstrates "how the rising and setting of constellations were used as a calendrical guide to agricultural events, from which were drawn mundane astrological predictions," for example:

> Fifty days after the solstice, when the season of wearisome heat is come to an end, is the right time to go sailing. Then you will not wreck your ship, nor will the sea destroy the sailors, unless Poseidon the Earth-Shaker be set upon it, or Zeus, the king of the deathless gods (II. 663-677).

And this was already ancient knowledge by Hesiod's time: lunar cycles were being charted as early as 25,000 years ago, the first step towards recording the Moon's influence upon tides and rivers, and towards organizing a communal calendar. The agricultural revolution brought increasing knowledge of constellations, whose appearances in the night-time sky change with the seasons, allowing the rising of particular star-groups to herald annual floods or seasonal activities. And this preview of astrology, along with a certain crabbiness, is a good summary of *Works and Days.* "As above, so below" wasn't just Hermetic esoteric doctrine: what was happening in the environment had direct influence on what was happening in their psyches. And that's basically what the concept of "embedded cognition" means: that the brain, and rationality, aren't the only cognitive resources at our disposal.

Again, it's beyond the scope of this talk to rehearse the battle between the folks who believe this and their academic opponents, the cognitive psychologists, who believe that it's all in the mind, but that latter viewpoint is a holdover from Descartes doubting everything he could perceive with his senses, thus bringing about the mind-body split, which was no good for anyone. Embedded cognition believes that we actually have extremely high quality, direct perceptual access to the world, and emphasizes the role perception, action and the environment can play in our actions. I can tell one story about this; it concerns the Inuit tribe in the Canadian north, and comes from Nicholas Carr, one of our most famous skeptics of technology, in his book *The Glass Cage*.

He started this particular chapter by describing their environment: "The average temperature hovers around twenty degrees below zero. Thick sheets of sea ice cover the surrounding waters. The sun is absent. . . . landmarks are few, snow formations are in constant flux, and trails disappear overnight" (125). Because it was pretty much winter 365 days a year, the Inuit tribespeople had to develop "wayfinding" skills, to be able to know where they were going based on their knowledge of "winds, snowdrift patterns, animal behavior, stars, tides, and currents." This was an inherited knowledge and skill that was continuously taught and developed over thousands of years. But then, in the year 2000 or so, came the use of the global positioning system. And once GPS became popular, those trustworthy Inuit guides started having accidents: they relied too much on satellites; their feeling for the land weakened; they lost sight of their surroundings. And wayfinding, this singular talent of their tribe for thousands of years, wrote Carr, might evaporate over the course of one generation.

So what I would say to you is that this seems very much like the transition from orality to literacy, and very much like what's happening to all our memories from our overuse – or misuse – of technology. And it might be one reason why the Muses are so elusive these days.

Conclusion: The Muses and the Wild

The Muses' Contest with the Sirens (Marble sarcophgagus, 3rd quarter
of 3rd century A.D. Roman. The Metropolitan Museum of Art, New York)

I mentioned at the beginning the publicity for this talk on the
Centre website, part of which raised the question, "Are the Muses
Still Around?"

> Some people say the muses are imaginary, and that's true: more
> true than when an inspired artist labels this or that person a muse.
> But the muses are invisible; they're never more than sojourners in
> our realm, and we in theirs. But we can sense them, every so often,
> even though we don't speak their language (that's actually why we
> need them). As Wordsworth wrote (not about them), "They're an
> amplitude of mind." Or as Dante had it, in the *Inferno,* "poet   by
> the God you did not know   lead on."

The great Islamist scholar Henry Corbin, in a lecture from 1974,
spoke about this as well:

> Saving the appearances: what does this mean? The phenomenon
> is that which shows itself, that which is apparent and which in
> its appearance shows forth something which can reveal itself . . .
> only by remaining concealed beneath the appearance. Something
> shows itself in the phenomenon and can show itself there only by
> remaining hidden.

I can't think of a better description of how the Muses work. And of
course, when things are hidden, there's mystery, or bewilderment,
here recalling a previous Centre session on the wild by William

Rowlandson. The definition of "bewilder" is to "confuse as to direction or situation"; my faithful 1961 Websters dictionary suggests "to cause to lose one's bearings" . . . which is, I think, a necessary prelude to any sort of creativity: to get lost, not seeing anything familiar, is potentially to see the new. Likewise, "wild" – living in a state of nature, not domesticated; growing, produced, or prepared without the aid and care of man, not cultivated; not inhabited; uncivilized. Because in these matters, there's no guarantee: what's unknown is best. As the Greeks knew, the truth is always a mystery.

So a start to summoning the muses might be to get out of our own way, to de-emphasize ourselves and pay more attention to what's going on around us. "'When humans aren't center stage,' writes environmental geographer Jamie Lorimer, 'the expertise of animals is valued, and organisms and landscapes are given more scope to determine their own futures.' A knotty, weedy wild is produced, in which ecology is allowed a kind of agency, and biodiversity is restored."

This chimes with the fact that while the muses are personifications, they're not exactly human. They may be invisible, but the works they support become visible; they "bubble up," as in the birth of the soul. It's also smart to figure out what's blocking them (usually, thinking too much, or depending too much on rationality). So I'll close with a few questions, after calming the mind, and letting our imaginations breathe – remembering that the word "soothe" has close relations to "sooth" – what is it that the Muses need? What in us is necessary for them? The answers we come up with will determine whether we can still hear their singing.

About the Author

Joe Safdie's ninth book was *The Secular Divine,* a hybrid chapbook of poems with an essay on heresy (Spuyten Duyvil, 2022). That essay gave its name to a collection of other essays on literary matters, *Poetry and Heresy,* forthcoming this year from MadHat Press (the essay "Musing about the Muses" is also in that volume). His talks on the muses and William Blake can be found on the website of the Centre for Myth, Cosmology and the Sacred in London, and his talk on Charles Olson and Brooks Adams for the American Literature Association can be found in *Spoke IX* and on YouTube. Other poems, essays, and reviews are in *Jacket, Jacket2, spoke, Rain Taxi, Caesura,* and *Dispatches from the Poetry Wars.* With his wife Sara and his cat Cody, he lives among the trees in Portland, Oregon.

About Chax Press

Founded in 1984 in Tucson, Arizona, Chax has published more than 250 books in a variety of formats, including hand printed letterpress books and chapbooks, hybrid chapbooks, book arts editions, and trade paperback editions such as the book you are holding. From August 2014 until July 2018 Chax Press resided in the University of Houston-Victoria Downtown Center for the Arts. Chax is a nonprofit 501c3 organization which depends on suppport from various government & private funders, and, primarily, from individual donors and readers. In July 2018 Chax Press returned to Tucson. In 2021, Chax Press founder and director Charles Alexander was awarded the Lord Nose Award for lifetime achievement in literary publishing. In January 2024 Chax established a new studio for its letterpress printing and book arts work.

Our current mailing address is 1517 North Wilmot Road no. 264, Tucson, Arizona 85712-4410. You can email us at *chaxpress@chax.org*

Your support of our projects as a reader, and as a benefactor, is much appreciated.

Find CHAX online at *https://chax.org*

Ελληνικά για μένα / Greek to Me
has been composed in Athelas and Gill Sans

Design by Charles Alexander

Printed & Bound by KC Book Manufacturing